What's the Time Mr. Wolf?

Jenny Feely

🦴 **Dominie Press, Inc.**

Let's play a game.

What's the time Mr. Wolf?

0 1 2 3 4 5 6 7 8 9 10

Two o'clock

0 1 **2** 3 4 5 6 7 8 9 10

What's the time Mr. Wolf?

0 1 2 3 4 5 6 7 8 9 10

Four o'clock

0 1 2 3 **4** 5 6 7 8 9 10

What's the time Mr. Wolf?

0 1 2 3 4 5 6 7 8 9 10

Dinner time!

0 1 2 3 4 5 **6** 7 8 9 10